First Things When

ROBERT REHDER was born and grew up in eastern Iowa. He attended Princeton, where he majored in Near Eastern studies. He studied at the École des langues orientales in Paris and at the University of Tehran, then returned to Princeton to do a PhD in Near Eastern studies. He has worked as a checkroom attendant, private dining-room waiter, painter, busboy, gardener, picked apples, polished silver, taught English composition at Princeton, English grammar in Tehran and ice-skating in a nursery school. He lived for a couple of years in Tehran, travelled to Afghanistan, across Turkey and around Iran. He crossed the Dasht-i Kavir and Dasht-i Lut, the big deserts of eastern Iran, making the first scientific collection of the plants in the area for Kew Gardens.

For a number of years he was Professor of English and American literature at the University of Fribourg in French-speaking Switzerland, where he lived in the small village of Corminboeuf.

Also by Robert Rehder from Carcanet Press

The Compromises Will Be Different

ROBERT REHDER

First Things When

CARCANET

Acknowledgements

Grateful acknowledgement is made to the following publications, in which some of the poems in this book first appeared:

The Iowa Review: 'Open Letter to the Secretary of the Swedish Academy', 'Free Fall', 'Archipelago'.

The Poet's Voice: 'White on White', 'Farmers' Market', 'Corminboeuf 797', 'Queequeg in His Coffin'.

PN Review: 'Habeas Corpus', 'The Gam', 'Yellow'.

First published in Great Britain in 2009 by
Carcanet Press Limited
Alliance House
Cross Street
Manchester M2 7AQ

A CIP catalogue record for this book is available from the British Library
ISBN 978 1 85754 909 6

The publisher acknowledges financial assistance from Arts Council England

Typeset by XL Publishing Services, Tiverton
Printed and bound in England by SRP Ltd, Exeter

Contents

Snow

Back in the USA

The World Elsewhere

And What Should I Do in Illyria?

Snow

In Media Res

The snow sifts the evidence
Without coming to a conclusion.

The value of sadness
Has yet to be established.

On the fruit trees
You cannot distinguish

The blossom
From the snow.

Our desires count for nothing.
The world is translated,

The text,
Downloaded.

Too late, we learn that
This is the Promised Land.

Snowfall

The carnival is over
And the masks are laid aside –

Drifts of confetti in every corner.
The world is white,

As if Locke were right,
The illusion of a new beginning,

But there is no reason
To believe in anything.

Habeas Corpus

The first snowfall asks questions
That are not answered,

Dusting everything white,
Leaving us to rethink our purposes.

Who needs more description?
The American Revolution might have

Turned out differently.
The British government did not understand

The American reality.
They lost touch.

And the generals were too slow,
Too careful, too indecisive,

And unwilling to take risks.
They did everything by the book.

I keep putting off writing letters,
Writing is so final.

I do not want the moment to end.
The snow is a repetition of some old event,

Transformation,
Memory or draped figure,

A past that returns.
This is why we understand things,

The only way.
As you grow older, you can be freer,

Not caring is almost like freedom,
And there are fewer choices.

When the Music Stops

The snow puts nothing away,
Discards all its cards

And throws its clothes on the floor –
Piano with no black keys.

There is no story.
The snow falls

And falls,
Until it has had enough.

Stay put
And you still change.

Tabula Rasa

The snow turns the page.
The familiar disappears.

History is an illusion.
We are distracted

By more important concerns
As the snow continues,

Spending millions on research,
Talking us down

To a soft landing.
No one has been here before.

Free Fall

Having learned nothing from experience,
The snow keeps coming,

Trying to be everywhere at once
And jumping to conclusions –

Rush hour,
The traffic is backed up for miles.

A peacekeeping force occupies the capital
And makes a house-to-house search.

We've lost our place in the book
And cannot find it.

The snow has something to say
About everything

And rushes into the present
As if it were coming home.

Après moi, le déluge

The snow has decided not to wait.
It hurries down

With all the disorder
Of my helter-skelter life,

Burying the world in uncertainty.
We are determined

To go on as before
And resist any simplification,

The whiter-than-paper brilliance
Of the new-fallen nearness.

Carte Blanche

The snow offers
A new vocabulary in which

To discuss our lives
That are largely unexpressed

And about which we find
Almost nothing to say –

White silence,
Each flake, a memory.

Imagine a language made only
Out of your experience.

The New World Is the Old World

The snow repeats itself.
The explanation is never finished.

We do not completely understand
And are where we always are,

Between approximations.
Now, surrounded by

The familiar strangeness
Of its subdued, used gaudiness

And throwaway glitter,
The cold events

Returning as if repressed,
We do not recognize ourselves in a world

Submerged in white words,
Crystal obscure.

Again

Snow, again –
And more snow.

The world is being packed
For shipment.

The flakes wander down
As if the rules have been changed –

Slowly,
Hanging back,

Children, reluctant to come in from play.
New snow covers the old,

Gravity's gift.
Yesterday's lesson is erased.

Things disappear –
The price of renewal.

Year's End

The snow has come back,
An event between remembering

And forgetting.
There were no promises,

Simply an understanding.
We didn't think

That it would be like this.
We wished for something different.

The snow has no childhood to play out.
It does what it wants.

The forest doesn't look the same.
We do not recognize ourselves.

We have trouble finding our way.
There's never time to finish anything.

You want to turn the corner
And never get to the end of the block.

Home Truths

Mid-April and it's been snowing
For three days.

Every tree is a fruit tree.
The snow prefers the status quo ante

And sets the clock back.
The violets are gone, primroses,

And tulips –
Nostalgia,

Entropy?
Unable to come to terms with the past,

Disorganized,
Out of phase with itself,

The snow hesitates in its hurry
To get home.

White on White

The snow fills the hollow sky:
Visible music,

Falling stars.
I have been here before.

Slowly whirling
At the edge of the light,

The snow is a novel in code
Blown off its pages

Never to be reconstructed,
Floating ruins,

Obsession,
Irresistible truths.

Everything is as if remembered.
I am still dreaming

Of a different world in which
There is more time –

Although the decisions
Have been taken.

Back in the USA

Hi There

Here we are, on my old stamping grounds,
The whole family,

Me, Caroline and Katherine,
Enjoying the excitement

Of shopping after dark at K-mart
And hearing people talk about internet.

We breakfast at the Hy-Vee
Where you have to give your first name

To get your breakfast –
Democracy is so intimate.

As I was buying an air ticket in the mall,
My travel agent, Annette,

We've never dated
And had only met on the telephone,

She's looking into my eyes,
Murmuring: "Bear with me, Robert,

I'll be right with you,"
Although she was only talking into her headset

On the other side of her desk,
Trying to get me a consolidator for Zürich.

Think of it:
Two hundred and sixty million people

On a first-name basis,
What are they trying to hide?

The action is somewhere else,
Which is why everyone walks around plugged into earphones.

They all wear Reeboks
So they can start running

As soon as they get the message.
Maybe this explains fast food.

Who can afford to think?
They don't invite each other to dinner

Because they're too busy,
Instead of friends you have email.

After three weeks, Caroline said:
"It's a siege mentality."

We need high crime rates,
They confirm that we're threatened.

We work all the time,
Because nothing has any meaning.

Ranch

When I asked the young woman
Behind the counter at the Hy-Vee:

"What is that?"
She said: "Chop-chop."

And we experienced a moment
Of total non-communication.

As she did not look like an Asian in a hurry
And discounting the possibility

That this was a new form of ethnic slur,
I repeated the question:

"I mean, what is it?"
"It's broccoli, carrots, cauliflower…"

I could see that it was broccoli and friends,
What I was concerned about

Was the white sauce
In which they were swimming,

Creatures from the pale lagoon.
Maybe they were going to paint the Hy-Vee

Using natural colours
Or the Titanic had sunk

And the only survivors were vegetables.
I was certain there were better ways

Of getting broccoli clean.
"What is the dressing?"

"Ranch."
I couldn't have been more surprised

If she had started to sing "Home on the Range."
Where did this masked rider come from?

This is Iowa. We don't do ranches,
We have farms.

You're not going to tell me
That Wyatt Earp put this stuff on lettuce?

And Buffalo Bill?
When I was young we went every summer

To Colorado
And no one ever mentioned ranch dressing.

This is our all-American nostalgia
For a past that never existed.

You're not going to believe what happened next.
For some time now you've had your doubts

About me
And you're right.

This is the payoff: I ordered a portion.
Why am I so crazy,

Is it because I was born here?
If people cared about what they ate

Would the streets be safer?
So I'm eating this stuff

That tastes like watered down cold cream,
Wondering if you can outgrow masochism

And whether it's more democratic
To have no standards.

Do you ever think that your life
Hasn't turned out the way you anticipated −

Which means, of course, that you're somebody else.
Americans don't understand cities.

Despite our desire to fix everything,
We can't make them work,

But it takes a truly great nation
To ruin salad.

Farmers' Market

What do you do when you meet a rhubarb pie
And it says "Smile" on it?

There I am in the farmers' market,
Minding my own business,

And there's this pie, communicating.
I didn't want to be rude,

But that's the kind of thing that pisses me off.
You don't always know how to respond.

I have the good old American reaction:
Kick it in the face.

What was the number of the last Rocky movie?
I lost track

And was it *Superman 6*?
We have this problem in the United States

With our emotions.
They're dirty

(Don't misunderstand me, everybody's are),
And we can't accept that,

Which is why we invented political correctness
And California.

Now nobody has to be real ever again.
That's why you have all these pies

Belonging to the religious right.
Of course, you know where they hold

The farmers' market in Iowa City?
On the ground floor of a parking garage.

Talk about denial.
If we sell organic vegetables here,

That'll show 'em who's boss.
Then, too, it has that macho,

Clandestine aura,
Like you were selling drugs, guns

Or meeting Deep Throat.
The University interviewed this guy

To teach contemporary British,
He hadn't been there,

Showed clips from a movie that
Even the people who say *film* thought was boring,

Couldn't answer the questions,
So they hired him.

It was either that or judge him –
They had no way out.

I had fewer problems with "Good Morning"
And "I Love You"

On the blackberry,
At least, it wasn't telling me what to do.

Melt Down

What's happening in America?
No one can believe in anything.

When the best restaurant in Charleston
Puts chocolate in the pecan pie,

You know you're in deep trouble,
But it doesn't stop there,

It doesn't stop anywhere.
There are no limits.

English departments no longer
Want to teach literature

And nobody thinks twice about saying
One-parent family.

At the New Pioneer in Iowa City
They put curry powder in the hummus,

Raspberry jam in the cinnamon rolls,
And it might easily have gone the other way.

It's a potlatch mentality,
The baker's dozen out of control,

A multi-media approach –
As if Mies van der Rohe had never lived.

Ray Charles is in *The World Book*
And can you believe, Martin Scorsese?

You get Dr. Seuss, but no Madame de Sevigné.
We don't know what anything is.

No wonder no one wants to discipline their children,
Much less themselves.

You go to a restaurant
And they have the television on –

Sometimes half a dozen sets tuned
To different channels.

We don't know when to stop.
It's not that we have no tradition –

This is it!
To bring the Statue of Liberty up to date,

We're going to junk the torch
And replace it with a tuna melt.

Go West

The end of the world has started
In the Tri-Cities

Of eastern Washington,
Kennewick, Richland and Pasco,

Where the aesthetic is not a category.
You cannot buy a newspaper

At the Columbia Center mall in Kennewick.
We're not here to learn.

The black girl in the bookstore
Stacked high with bestsellers says:

"You might try a grocery store"
On the assumption, I suppose,

That perishables belong together,
But there's not one of them either,

And no restaurant
Where you can sit down to eat.

The mall exists to sell us what we don't need.
Whatever happened to beauty?

Crowds of sedentary people in sports clothes
Wander about

Admiring the brand new desolation
That gives a new meaning

To the cost of living.
Being here is like appearing on television.

This is a city composed of suburbs.
They have moved to the country to destroy it,

Put their children into day care
And spend more time in their cars.

This is a phantasy world
Superimposed with an absolute disregard

For the landscape.
Nothing belongs,

An in-your-face ugliness
That insists

On the unconditional surrender
Of the natural world.

We're always doing this.
The bulldozers are out there now

Scratching the itch.
Do we hate our mothers so much?

Star Wars

Let's get a few things straight.
I was against it from the start.

It wasn't my idea.
I didn't want the video.

Caroline thought it would be good
For our French (she was right).

I knew what would happen.
Talk about fatal attraction!

She is strong
And self-disciplined –

I don't know the meaning of the word.
She is one of those people

Who do what they say.
I have no will power.

I think about Brad Pitt –
Stop.

Does any more need to be said, I mean, is this
The life of a grown up? –

And I wait for Julia Roberts to smile,
Like she does when she decides

To enjoy the polo in *Pretty Woman*.
The images replay themselves

As if they were my experience.
It's the invasion of the body snatchers –

I haven't even seen that one and I know about it!
I worry

Whether the chemical factory in *I Love Trouble* is
The same set as in *Demolition Man*.

I brood over this as if I were Proust.
I notice the bags under Meg Ryan's eyes in *French Kiss*

As they sit in the café
Before Kevin Kline's brother, Antoine, arrives

Which are gone
When she appears in the soft blue dress

To go to dinner with Charlie.
From *Striptease*, it is clear –

You can tell by the upper arm and shoulder muscles –
That since *Ghost*

Demi Moore's been working out more.
I never finished the biography of Chamfort

And am still in Book II of Locke's *Essay*.
I have given up writing letters.

My life is out of control.
I neglect Prokofiev.

Without trying, I pick up on
What *Bounty Hunters* lifted

From *Lethal Weapon 3*.
Have you ever heard of these movies?

These details are probably lost on you
And in a hundred years

They're going to drive the scholars crazy.
They're driving me crazy now.

Things might be different if my life had a purpose.
Forget de Tocqueville, never mind reality,

To explain American life
I use the scene in *The Specialist*

When Stallone throws the heavy metal nazi punk
Through the bus window

Because he takes the pregnant black woman's seat,
Although all the time I'm thinking

That for sheer elegance
It can't compare to when Jean-Claude destroys

The guys who are bothering the girl in the car
Outside the restaurant in *Hard Target*.

Of course, it was a really smart idea
To do the sequence in slow motion

So that it's almost a ballet,
Van Damme has all the moves –

Better than Seagal laying out the bandit
Who's robbing his neighborhood grocery in *Hard to Kill*,

Better than anything in *Sudden Death* or *Maximum Risk*.
The trouble is I could go on.

That's the problem.
There are worse things:

Television, death, shopping in malls.
I'm pretending this is purgatory,

But I'm runnin' on empty.
This poem has been modified

From its original version.
It has been formatted to fit your screen.

Queequeg in His Coffin

Take it from the top.
Depression, obsession, who cares?

My life is not my own.
I have this encyclopaedic knowledge

Of stuff I don't want to know.
The station

Where Kate and Luke get off the train in *French Kiss*
Is La Ravelle.

Waterworld is *Mad Max* at sea.
Johnny Mnemonic — wow, what a bad movie! —

Derives from *Cyborg* and *Blade Runner*.
All these crazy visions of the future

Are not as crazy as what's going on here.
The whole underground underworld business

Of *Blade Runner*
(They borrowed the title from Burroughs)

Is all over the place:
Demolition Man, Highlander, Highlander 2.

The threat is from the unconscious,
Except in *Terminator*

Where the unconscious is our freedom,
And there's some of that in the others, too,

Now that I think of it —
Freedom is always a danger.

Johnny has my problem.
He's trying to download a bunch of memory

That's not his and he can't stand.
You see what I mean,

Before you know it, you're involved.
The Rodeo Drive boutique in which

The two awful saleswomen snub Julia Roberts
Is called Boule Miche.

There are only a few frames in *Pretty Woman*
Where you can read it

Backwards, in white translucent block caps,
On the window over the door.

I hope I've impressed you
With the range and futility of my knowledge.

Ice T was enough of a success in *Johnny Mnemonic*
That they've done a remake of *Hard Target*,

Surviving the Game, with him in Jean-Claude's part.
No, I haven't seen it yet,

But word gets around.
Do you recognize me as the man

Who has read
Turkestan Down to the Mongol Invasion

Very carefully, twice?
(I think I still have my notes somewhere).

I like the movies where guys triumph
Against the odds

And I'll probably be watching one
When I die.

This is a piano sonata

This is a piano sonata.
You're bored with movie poems.

Me, too.
Would anyone watch *Beverly Hills Cowgirl's Blues*

Eight times (and it's not over)
If they weren't in serious trouble?

Everybody's life looks better at a distance,
But I'm tired of tossing salad.

"Nothing is more reasonable than boredom,"
So Leopardi

Who changed his shirt once a month
And found his pleasure eating ice cream.

Talk about ephemera.
If I said I was reading the Comtesse de Boigne

Would you be better off?
Or Olaudah Equiano?

Movies are easier than ice cream.
The world comes to you

And you don't have to do anything.
They support this imaginary life I'm leading

A little to one side of reality.
"To me he is as much a riddle –

I might almost say as much a stranger –
As he was twenty-five years ago."

And Clara knew Brahms better than anyone.
Imagination is the only freedom.

Maybe not –
The day's events return in tonight's dreams.

Our choices overtake us
Like semis on the highway.

The Frontier

Lemme tell you about Cultural Studies,
The new American craziness.

At Wisconsin there's this professor
Who studies border art

Which is when a Mexican sneaks into the US
Does a graffito – social context is crucial –

Paints a picture, whatever.
Any of our guys sneak into Mexico,

It doesn't count –
Wouldn't be multicultural.

If a Mexican paints a picture in Mexico,
It's no go. Where's the art?

If he paints in Tucson or El Paso,
But on the way has his passport stamped,

Forget it.
The work has no intellectual interest.

If your back isn't wet, it's not border art.
There's this incredible quality you get

If the artist has been baptized in the Rio Grande,
Hidden under burlap sacks

Or in a truckload of melons.
Can you spell *silly*?

Lucia was in the locker room changing
When a class of freshman women came in

Talking about what they were taking.
This is Illinois.

English, history, sociology, communications –
At the end of the semester, in every subject,

They were going to analyze a Madonna video.
Wow! What a preparation for life!

If you can analyze a Madonna video,
You may be smart enough

To watch television all by yourself.
And since the teenies haven't listened

To what's-her-name for years,
It's really neat for Cultural Studies to have this classic icon,

You know, like Plato or Thomas Jefferson,
So that the kids have a sense of the tradition.

Over in Germany, they're cool, too.
Her friends in American literature, Pia says,

Are doing a project on the Simpsons.
(Didn't they write *Moby-Dick*?)

And I met this guy in Iowa
Whose academic field of interest is shopping malls.

Yes, of course, he's in English.
They don't do stuff like that in business schools.

English is where it's at.
But Thursday

Was breakthrough day.
Recognizing that in an era

Of techno-globalism,
Following the post-mall interregnum,

There would be a need for a more focused,
Upscale,

Erudition-deficient, consumer-oriented topic,
Open to free-association Lacanian discourse

And Benjaminian object theory,
Combining straight-up Stuart Wilson narrative

With Homi Bhabha babble,
I thought it was time to turn the other *chic*,

So at lunch,
I invented boutique studies,

Because of which I am going to be intensely famous
For the next eight months.

I've got this grant to do research in Palm Springs
And Beverly Hills,

The grant proposal is being published in *Social Text*
And *People* magazine has asked for an interview.

That's the wonderful thing
About Cultural Studies,

You stop thinking
And have all these great ideas.

Excuse Me?

Kelly Preston, Kelly McGillis, Kelly Lynch –
Gene Kelly,

You have to respect the differences.
Does your right hand know

What your left hand is doing?
There is Kristy Swanson

And Kirsty Alley,
Not to be confused with Ally Sheedy

Who is so great in *The Breakfast Club*,
Not to mention Kristin Scott Thomas.

Reality is not easy. Who are you?
Beethoven's first piano concerto

Is the second.
Brahms' second piano sonata is his first.

Hadrian is the first Roman emperor
To have a beard.

Who said anything about happiness?
Nobody knows in what order

Haydn composed his Opus 33.
Who can you trust?

The fear of breaking down is the fear
Of what has already happened.

Loneliness is a memory.
As they say in Mississippi:

"The delta begins in the lobby
Of the Peabody Hotel in Memphis."

Personal Best

"Another way to put *that* question is to ask what happens next, what psychological poets should do once they have exhausted their best personal material, should they spy on other people to generate new drama in their lives? Or delve for new conceptions of poetry, ones which won't depend on revealing deep secrets?"

What happens next? Psychological poets?
Are there any other kind?

This isn't the rainbow coalition.
Steve is with Louise in her garage.

He's lost.
Your experience is all you have.

The subject is never over.
She's taking out the garbage

And wondering why her marriage failed.
Every statement is a metaphor.

She'll think about this for the rest of her life,
Because that's what we do.

Exhausted is when you keep trying
To change your life and don't.

There is no way she can avoid
Returning to what happened.

Nostalgia is our response to loss.
I'm really not up for any new drama.

Where is Aeschylus now that we need him?
My life is difficult enough.

You understand other people in so far
As you understand yourself.

The moment is never right.
Total honesty is not

What we're going to end up with,
Any more than we can save the earth.

The new ideas come from the same old things.
The trouble is we've been here before.

There are no secrets,
Only what we knew all along

And couldn't face.
It's there for the thinking. Help yourself.

The citation is from Stephen somebody's review
Of a book by Louise Glück.

I've lost the reference.
All roads lead to Damascus. Or Corminboeuf.

The World Elsewhere

Corminboeuf is a small village, originally a Roman farmstead, in French-speaking Switzerland, with some 1,200 people and 750 cows. Cows are counted in the Swiss census.

Corminboeuf IX

The story of the world-famous Corminboeuf poems
Has yet to be told.

I was sitting in my study wondering
Why

I was not at the center of the action
(A self-revelation if ever there was one)

And wishing
That I was in New York

Or Boston or even Los Angeles,
When I remembered –

There's nothing harder to accept than reality –
That I live in Corminboeuf.

Lesley Blanch was married
To the novelist Romain Gary,

Who was then
The French Ambassador

To Switzerland.
She left him, she said,

Because Bern was so boring
She couldn't stand it any longer.

Caroline often threatens
To run away to Bern.

My life has its downs and downs

My life has its downs and downs.
Basically, there's not enough future

And I'm living a phantasy.
Who needs tragedy?

Reality, I've been there.
This is no time to be imagining

What you would do if you were free
Or rich

Or could start from somewhere else.
Too late for a Walden.

Everything takes longer than we plan.
The forest is full of last year's leaves.

Sometimes I don't listen to music,
Because I know how long it will last.

Today is my birthday.
Yeah? Thanks.

I'm bored out of my mind.
Are you waiting for something, too?

Our plans to go away collapsed
And July it rained every day.

There is nothing to do
Except what I usually do

Which is nothing.
The best that Caroline could come up with

Is to spray the evergreens for the red spider.
I wanted to have a party,

But the trouble with Switzerland is
There are no people,

And the trouble with sentences that begin
"The trouble with" is

That they don't go anywhere.
We already know everything is difficult.

Now, it's hot,
At least when it's hot in Iowa

You're in Iowa.
There didn't seem any point to a cake,

I'd only have to work to lose the weight tomorrow
And for once I didn't feel like drinking

A whole bottle of champagne by myself.
This is called living for the moment.

I am so bored
The only thing I can find to do is write poetry.

Why isn't every day a poem?
If you have to ask what's important,

You're lost.
All we have in Corminboeuf is choices.

I wanted a chocolate cake,
Only I couldn't bring myself to ask for one.

Not Expression, Endurance

I like the slow movements best,
Gray pearls

That look slightly veiled.
They hold more together,

Half tones,
Sadness – stepping stones, unfinished bridge.

Experience is what is left over,
The residue, intermezzo,

Life savings.
There is no lullaby for all our griefs.

Archipelago

This happens in Schubert
And elsewhere,

Iowa, for example.
There is something incomplete that lingers,

Trails off
And a pause –

That lengthens
And goes on – and on.

Strand by strand,
The rope breaks.

The fingertips cannot remember
The last thing they touched.

The boat pulls away from the dock –
The old confusion

Between forgetting and loss.
Then a series of notes played more slowly,

Softer,
Echoing – remotely, precisely –

The previous phrase,
Almost a melody,

On the edge –
A very slow waterfall

Suggesting completeness,
Gifts

Exchanged
In the interstices of the stars.

Canyon de Chelly

From the rim you go down
A tunnel

Through the solid rock
To where the wall falls away

Gradually,
Fans out

As if poured,
The rounded steps

Of a giant stair,
Stone waterfall,

Rusted, pink and buff,
Work in progress,

The appearance of permanence,
To which the sparse, tenacious juniper

And piñon cling,
Growing from the cracks

And breaking the rock.
You zigzag and switchback

Around massive boulders,
Along obdurate edges,

Down over the billowing sandstone,
Like walking on a piece of sculpture,

Down to the canyon floor,
Tawny sand, river and White House –

Built on the cliff shelf
And below, under the cottonwoods,

Ruins,
Yesterday,

Another kind of silence,
A language no one can remember.

Our destinations are never final.
The past has no beginning.

Chaco

The great houses of Chetro Ketl
And Pueblo Bonito

Are empty.
The roofs are gone.

The upper stories have fallen in.
As usual, we don't know what happened.

Events keep eluding us –
Ruins,

Our incompleteness.
The remaining walls

With their expert, intricate stonework
Are a triumph of desire,

Definite, clear-cut
And free standing.

The tawny canyon is the memory
Of an older river,

A clock set on geologic time,
Another ruin.

The only thing we find here
Is the present.

Temple Stream

The stream runs downhill
As if that were something new,

Finding instinctively
The shortest path, the steepest gradient,

Slashes across the slanted, jammed down
Granite slab,

Sheet of liquid glass that explodes,
Jagged scatter of shards,

The same explosion endlessly repeated –
Regathers,

Cuts between the dark, embedded boulders,
Boiling up,

White fire from a diver's torch.
We never see the whole,

Only parts,
Odd lengths of string in the kitchen drawer.

Continuity is imagined.
The stream builds a staircase to go down,

Music trying to find its way back
To the melody,

The past rushing
At every moment into the present.

Beginning

The past chooses our memories
And decides.

We repeat the strangeness.
We cross the bridge over the river

And are not connected to anything.
The flow of objects separates us

From ourselves.
First things when –

If only I could figure out what they are.
This is the space of absences.

The faint flowery perfume that hovers
Over my glass of Riesling is the vanishing frontier.

Evening lingers
And refracts green through the green stem,

Can our knowledge save us?
The wine, a gold shadow.

Yellow

The edge is always dangerous.
You're on your own.

Sulphur yellow

Why is the most inventive, radical American poetry
Being written in Corminboeuf?

Nickel yellow

The rain forest is nothing
Compared to the strangeness of our behaviour.

Naples yellow

Accepting responsibility
For our phantasies is where we fail.

Lemon yellow japanese

Jerry Fodor hates relativism
More than he hates anything

Strontium yellow

Except, maybe, fiberglass power boats.
I love hate

Flanders yellow

Which explains perhaps
My relations with disorder.

Cadmium yellow lemon

Corot said he began with the shadows.
Now I want to rebuild,

Zinc yellow

But I'm in a hurry and unable to start.
The early years decide for you.

Helium yellow

The world is the way it is
And you might as well get used to it,

Cadmium yellow pale

I can't.
I imagine

Chrome yellow light

That I can do everything in a nanosecond
By thinking about it.

Japanese yellow light

My routine is to make a schedule
And break it.

Senegal yellow

And I've broken two mugs.
When I reach out

Cadmium yellow light

To put them down,
I rest them mostly in midair.

Chrome yellow medium

They fall and break.
You're always fighting your family

Brilliant yellow

Whether you had one or not.
The dream is where we live.

Chrome yellow deep

The past is never past.
Every poem is paradise lost.

Sahara yellow

And What Should I Do in Illyria?

Open Letter to the Secretary of the Swedish Academy

Dear Sir,
Please send me a Nobel Prize.

I have completed the enclosed coupon
And attach three Quaker Puffed Wheat box tops.

The newspaper said that Mr. Heaney's prize was
Over a million dollars.

That would be satisfactory.
We could use the money.

Katherine wants a new horse,
Caroline would like to enlarge the kitchen

And I have this crazy idea
That I would like to live in my own country,

And since the UN Commissioner for Refugees
Is taking a long time

To get to my dossier,
I would spend some of the money to do that.

As the recent prizes for literature have been awarded
For political reasons,

I thought it would make a nice change
To give one simply for the poems,

And my poems are as simple
As I can make them (look at this one!).

The insouciance and naive charm
Of these notebook-aged compositions

With their toasty-oak nuances, supple tannins,
Sceptical overtones

And wild blackberry finish
Would doubtless be enhanced

By the award of a prize.
I would be happy to accept the prize for physics.

Reading Richard Feynman was the occasion
For one of my best poems –

As far as I know
The first poem ever written about a tea bag –

And no other poet in his own life
Has so exemplified chaos theory.

Feynman, as you remember, shared the prize in 1965
For his theory of the interaction

Of charged particles in a radiation field.
If, like most people, your budget's a bit tight,

I would not object to sharing a prize,
Medicine, for example, which is often shared,

Since my poems make people feel better –
And think.

If there was money left over
I would like to buy several square miles

Of rough pasture and woods in which to walk,
Maybe along the Cedar or Iowa rivers.

Every poet should possess a bit of wilderness.
You will have noticed that I have not said anything

About writing more poems.
Although the work of many winners

Has deteriorated markedly
After the award of their prizes,

It's a risk I'm prepared to take.
Frank says that in his experience

The easiest life crisis to cope with is success.
Anyway, you cannot write poems for money or prizes,

You can, but they don't last.
I'm hoping to go on as before,

But who knows what they're going to do next?
I write poems because I become restless,

Depressed,
Bad-tempered

And difficult to live with if I don't,
There's not another reason.

Infinity

Greenish at the base
The birches

Slashed with black
Are

Another colour than white
Washed with rose

Against
The snow.

No description describes them.
Approximation is not

What it's about.
You can't get there from here.

The Gam

Shshshsh, the Faculty is in session
And must not be disturbed.

This evening has been a showcase
Of dazzling virtuoso play.

When Professor Mortimer (always a popular speaker
Because he speaks to the point

And rarely longer than two minutes)
Moved to end debate,

The Faculty voted overwhelmingly in his favour,
The Dean, however,

Blithely went on calling on people
To discuss the original motion.

Professor Mortimer is the man
Who can be seen signalling over there on the right

Whom nobody notices,
Like a swimmer who has swum

Beyond the roped-off area
And disappears from sight.

For forty-five minutes we debated whether
We should suppress the program in social work,

When we were reminded we had already discussed this
Twice at previous meetings

And had decided to suppress it.
Then we spent another hour thinking

About restoring it,
Until someone explains: no,

What we are discussing is the way
That it is to be phased out.

Professor Z. intervenes to tell us how such things
Are settled in Italy

(Ribald chuckling from the middle of the table).
The worn out old guy near the door is Rehder,

The one who looks like he's suffering
From sensory deprivation.

Actually he's looking a little livelier tonight
As he's remembered to bring his copy of *Le Monde*.

Usually, he has that spaced-out look
Of those homeless bums

Who push their life
Around with them in a shopping cart.

They say he is the only professor in the Faculty
Who doesn't speak German.

I don't know why,
But the German speakers

Speak more often
And longer

Than the French speakers.
There was another, the very distinguished Professor of French

Who returned to Paris
As soon as he could afford it.

They used to compete for the seat closest to the door.
He would take out his bus timetable

Every five minutes or so,
As if he could endure to stay

Only if he was certain he could get home
At any moment.

Professor K. holds us spellbound
With an impassioned plea

To the effect that we cannot be such fools as to think
That we can teach theory and practice together

(He is German).
He disdainfully laughs away all objections.

A hush falls over the assembly
Indicating that sixty-eight out of seventy-three

Of those present
Have lost the thread of the argument

And that the five who know
Are too exhausted to care.

This is a very exciting moment,
Because it is the first time

That the Larsen Boredom Meter
Has been tested in a Swiss university.

Built by the Norwegian astrophysicist Eric Larsen,
During the winter he was snowbound in Antarctica,

The results of the field trials so far
Have been controversial

And there are hopes tonight of a new record.
The reading of 740

Taken at ten o'clock
On a Saturday night in downtown Zürich

Is still being contested.
Swiss scientists claim that any reading

Taken after six o'clock is unfair,
While experts at the International Board of Standards

Question whether there is a downtown Zürich.
Previous highs had been the 102

Recorded in Centennial, Wyoming
And the 119.5 registered at a motorway café

On the M1 outside Leeds.
"I told you," said the mayor of Centennial

When he heard the Swiss results,
"We're just peaceful here, not boring."

April in Krakow

These igloos are for recycling:
Green, glass, blue, paper, orange, metal.

You throw things away so that they return,
A boomerang system,

Green, glass, blue, paper, orange, metal,
Freud would have understood.

Bee basilicas – but the bees swarm elsewhere,
Trash banks, pantheons of the domestic,

Green, glass, blue, paper, orange, metal,
To commemorate unknown household soldiers,

Power stations on the river of samsara,
The Buddhism of objects,

Reincarnation, transmigration,
Green, glass, blue, paper, orange, metal,

Soft colours to soothe and encourage us
About the task of continuity.

If they look like playground playhouses,
It is due to the childishness

Of our behaviour when dealing with the world,
Green, glass, blue, paper, orange, metal.

Low domes, Eskimo and romanesque,
Hunters' camps,

Scattered throughout the city
Because caribou are scarce

Or the Inuit intuit
The presence of seals beneath the ice,

Green, glass, blue, paper, orange, metal,
Metal, orange, paper, blue, glass, green.

Untitled

Today's obsessions are tomorrow's truths.
You can get by on need.

The difficulty is finding what is there.
Simplicity is an act of analysis.

That which I should have I did not.
Everything is a sky.

Biographical

Black mussels in the black two-handed pot,
This is the real.
I want more than weather.

I have not finished Clement's *Chateaubriand*

If every day like Jefferson I wrote down
The temperature, air pressure and wind,
Would I be in charge of my life?

Pierrot's *Balzac*

The insides are bluish, white,
With smeared purple streaks from the sunset's end.
I don't want to go on waiting.

Swafford's *Brahms*

I'm tired of half-begun and never-finished.
Capitalize the losses.
They are the foundation of my world.

Black mussels in the black two-handed pot

Blue-black, black and black-lavender,
Dish of edges –
Every object is a frontier.

Entropy

The stillness of the city floats on
Unending movement –

Memory connected by forgetting.
On the Grand Canal I couldn't remember

The name of Michael Douglas's wife.
The ATM refuses your card.

What were we talking about?
Or Gianfranco's last name

And we had dinner with them last week.
The shabby, dilapidated palazzi

Have seen better days.
Or the author of the big book on Bellini

That I had had in my hands, where?
A few hours before. The Accademia.

The words we need elude us:
The fading splendour of an unknown world –

Secrets, passwords, return tickets.
We wander in the labyrinth

Of narrow streets, passageways, bridges
And dead ends – another Venice.

And What Should I Do in Illyria?

Fading splendour –
On the Grand Canal I forgot

Who plays Olivia –
an unknown,

Increasingly anonymous
world

That does not quite cohere
And nearly didn't remember Viola,

mossy stairs
Going down into the water.

Abruptly, the play which I know as well
As I know...

anything –
Sir Toby, Feste –

Disappears in the penumbra –
Disorder "is not an absolute,

But has meaning only in context" –
Vanishes,

Lost in the margins,
off stage,

And in the water-shine,
The restless, many-folded surface.

The city is delicately balanced
Upon the lagoon,

permanently at risk,
Words, empty museums.